Zuki's Beads

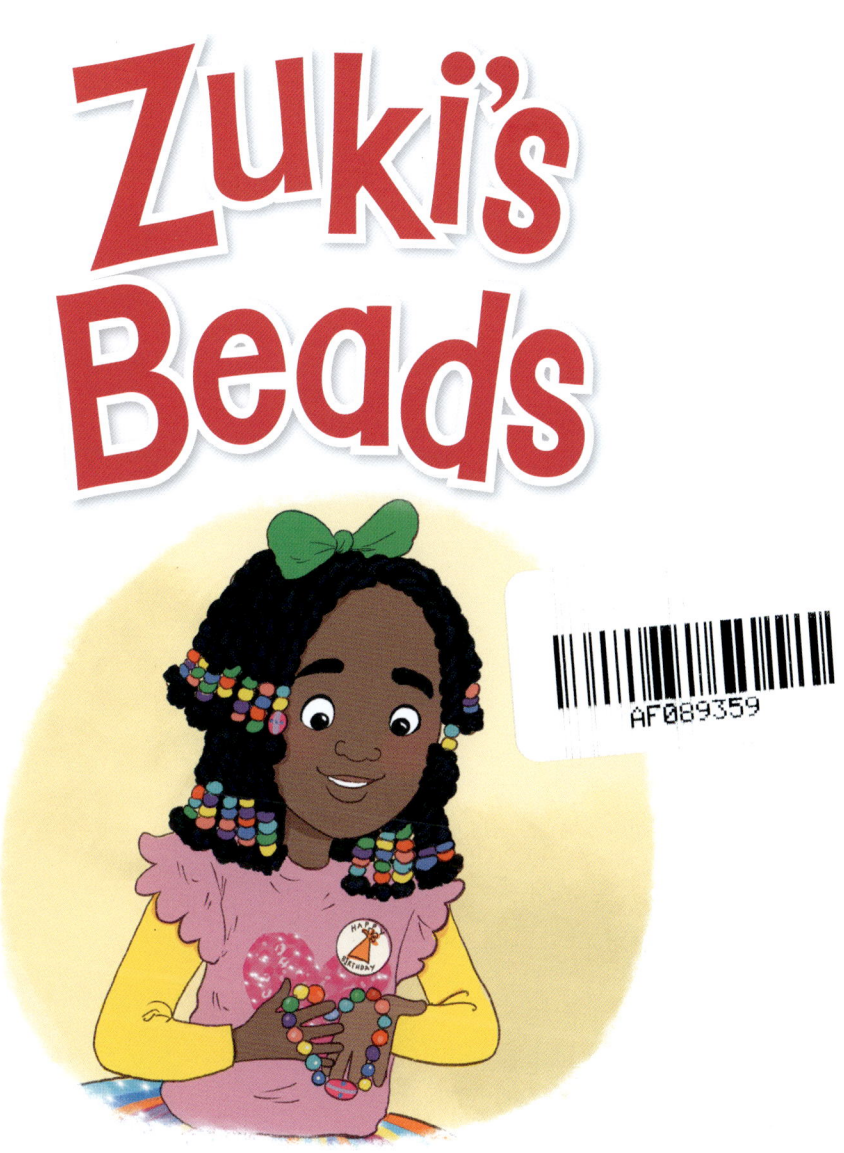

Written by Yelitza Smith
Illustrated by Rachel Moss

Collins

Every morning Zuki's mummy would sit and style her hair. Parting and twisting her afro with skilful speed and flair.

Sometimes she had two pigtails.

Sometimes she had four.

A twisted fringe.
An afro-puff.

A fluffy pompadour!

She'd always have two twisted braids,
with three beads on each side.
When Zuki wore her hair like this
she'd beam with so much pride.

The beads would swish, and click and clack
as Zuki moved her head.
So many different colours.
Yellow, purple, green and red.

One Monday morning Zuki woke
and looked down at her hair.
Only two beads on one side?
The third bead wasn't there!

A purple bead was missing!
But where could it have gone?
How could it have fallen off?
She'd had her bonnet on.

She always wore a bonnet
when she went to her bed.
Mum always reminded her
to put it on her head.

Sometimes the silky bonnet
would come off in the night.
When she woke in the morning
it was nowhere in sight.

But on that Monday morning
the bonnet was in place.
"Unusual!" Zuki noted,
then skipped off to wash her face.

On Wednesday, a blue one was missing!
Zuki thought, "Bizarre!
A purple? Now, a blue bead!
I wonder where they are."

The two beads still had not been found when Zuki went to bed.
"Don't worry, they will turn up soon," her mum had softly said.

Three weeks passed and more beads gone!
Things were getting weird.
Every time she went to sleep
another disappeared.

Zuki searched all round her room.
She'd started with the bed,
Found nothing by the pillow,
so checked the sheets instead.

She'd wondered if they'd rolled away,
so checked her bedroom floor.
She'd looked under the wardrobe
and searched behind the door.

She cried, "I cannot find them.
Oh, where could they have gone?
And if more beads go missing
then soon I will have none!"

Zuki's birthday arrived in June.
She was super excited!
Mum was making a special meal.
The whole family were invited.

Her nan arrived the night before
and brought a nice surprise.
Two beads that sparkled super bright
and dazzled Zuki's eyes.

Mum styled Zuki's hair that night,
ready for the big day.
"I won't have time tomorrow," she said,
tucking the braids away.

Zuki's hair looked wonderful.
The braids were extra neat.
But Zuki was worried about her beads
and struggled to fall asleep.

She woke up in the morning
and one of the beads was gone.

"Happy birthday, to the birthday girl!"
sang Dad and Nan and Mum.

Her family were dancing merrily.
"What's the matter?" asked her dad.
"Would you like to open your presents now?"
Zuki stood looking sad.

Her little brother stepped forward, holding a tiny gift.
"I'd used up all my pocket money, and so, I made you this."

Zuki smiled at her brother and said, "Don't worry, that's quite alright. Whatever you have made for me, I'm really sure I'll like."

The package was shaped quite oddly.
She opened it to find
the most beautiful, beaded necklace
folded up inside!

With every colour and every bead
that Zuki had ever lost.
And in the centre was the special bead
her nan gave her, of course.

"It was a surprise!" said her brother.
"To match your hair every day."

Zuki gasped and gave him a hug.
She didn't quite know what to say.

Zuki adored her necklace and
was delighted to have her beads back.
It matched all the beads in her hair.
As they swished, with a click and clack.

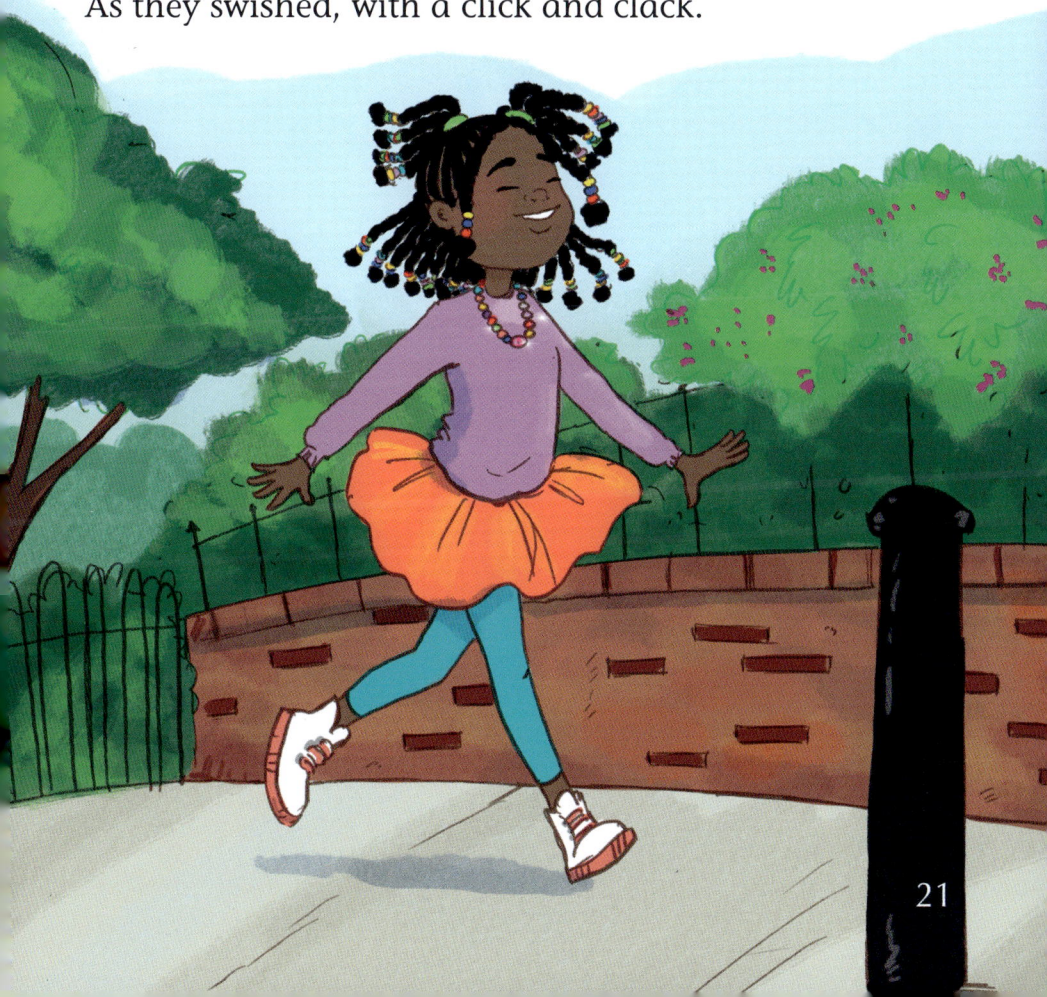

Finding the beads

Every morning Zuki's mummy would sit and style her hair.

Zuki adored her necklace and was delighted to have her beads back.

Her little brother stepped forward, holding a tiny gift.

"Would you like to open your presents now?" Zuki stood looking sad.

There were only two beads on one side! The third bead wasn't there!

Three weeks passed and more beads gone! Things were getting weird.

She'd wondered if they'd rolled away, so checked her bedroom floor.

Ideas for reading

Written by Gill Matthews
Primary Literacy Consultant

Reading objectives:
- discuss and clarify the meanings of words, linking new meanings to known vocabulary
- answer and ask questions
- predict what might happen on the basis of what has been read so far

Spoken language objectives:
- articulate and justify answers, arguments and opinions
- participate in discussions, presentations, performances, role play, improvisations and debates

Curriculum links: Relationships education: Families and people who care for me

Interest words: skilful, pride, weird, adored, delighted

Word count: 715

Resources: paper and pens

Build a context for reading

- Ask children to look at the front cover of the book and to read the title. Discuss what the title means to them.
- Read the back cover blurb and explain that this is a rhyming poem, pointing out the rhyming words in the blurb.
- Ask children what they think might happen in the story.

Understand and apply reading strategies

- Read pp2–5 aloud, using meaning and punctuation to help you read with appropriate expression. Discuss the features that make this a poem, and how this affects the way we read each line.
- Ask children to read pp6–9 aloud.
- Ask what they think might happen next in the story. Encourage children to support their responses with reasons and evidence from the text.